Requiem

for

FOUR-PART CHORUS OF MIXED VOICES
WITH SOPRANO AND BARITONE SOLI

by

Gabriel Fauré

Piano Reduction by
BRUCE HOWDEN

Orchestra parts are available on rental from the publisher.

This work is scored for 2 Flutes, 2 Clarinets in Bb, 2 Bassoons, 4 Horns in F, 2 Trumpets, 3 Trombones, Timpani, Harp, Organ, Strings.

Ed. 2243

A complete Organ Score, including all choral and solo passages, by Norris L. Stephens, is published.

G. SCHIRMER, *Inc.*

DISTRIBUTED BY
HAL•LEONARD®
CORPORATION
7777 W. BLUEMOUND RD. P.O. BOX 13819 MILWAUKEE, WI 53213

INDEX

REQUIEM

For Four-part Chorus of Mixed Voices
with Soprano and Baritone Soli and Piano Accompaniment

1. Introit and Kyrie
(Grant them rest eternal)

Gabriel Fauré, Op.48

43966c

1

2

on them,   shine down up — on   them.
e - is,   lu - ce - at   e -   is.

on them,   shine down up — on   them.
e - is,   lu - ce - at   e -   is.

on them,   shine down up — on   them.
e - is,   lu - ce - at   e -   is.

on them,   shine down up — on   them.
e - is,   lu - ce - at   e -   is.

Andante moderato ♩ = 72   Tenor   *dolce e espressivo*   p

Re - qui - em   ae -
Grant   them rest   e -

ter - nam   do - na e - is   Do - mi - ne,
ter - nal;   grant   them, Lord,   e - ter - nal rest;

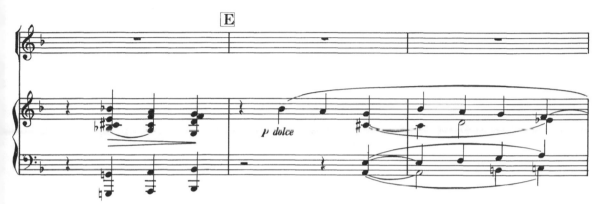

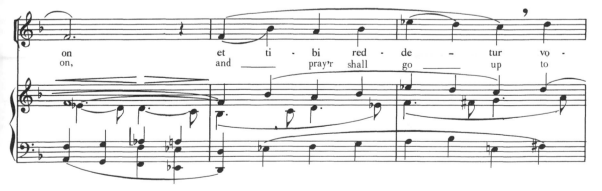

2. Offertory
(O Lord, our God)

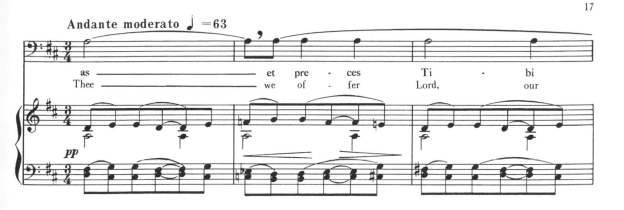

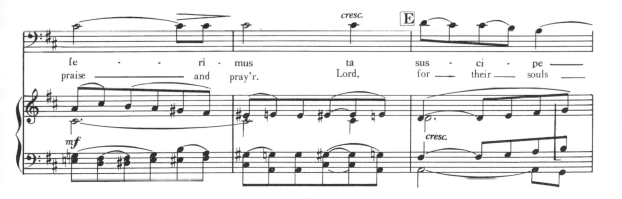

3. Sanctus

(Holy, Holy, Holy)

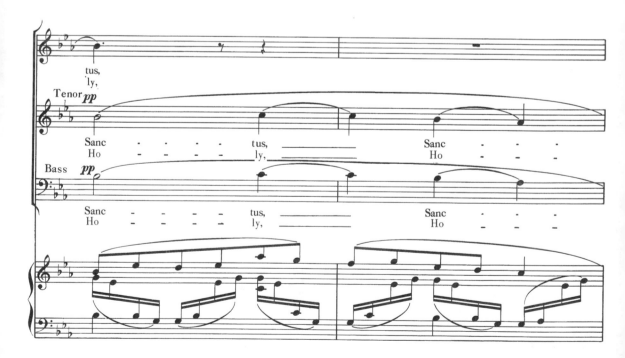

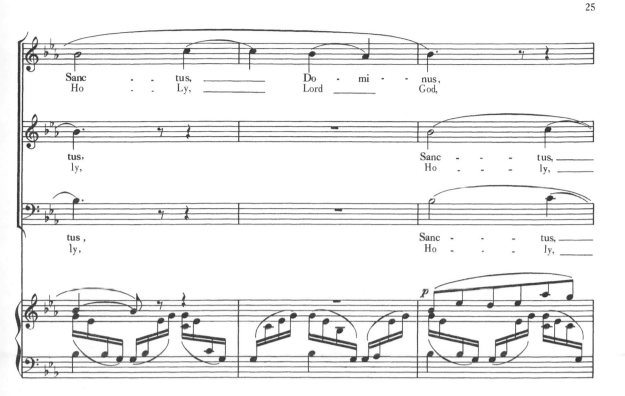

26

28

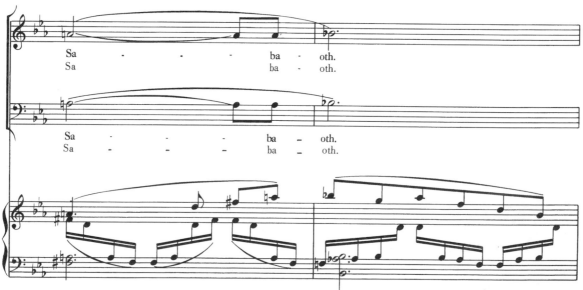

C *sempre dolce*

Soprano

Ple - ni sunt cae - li et
Heav - en and earth ___ are

ter - - - ra.
full of Thy glo - ry.

Tenor

Glo - ri - a, glo - ri - a
Glo - ry be, glo - ry be

sempre dolce
Bass

glo - ri - a, glo - ri - a
glo - ry be, glo - ry be

tu - a.
to Thee.

tu - a.
to Thee.

D

Soprano

p

Ho - san - na in _____ ex -
Ho - san - na in _____ the

cel - - - - sis,
high - - - - est,

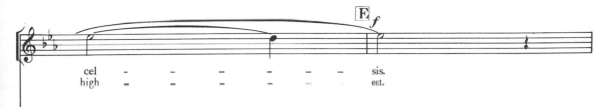

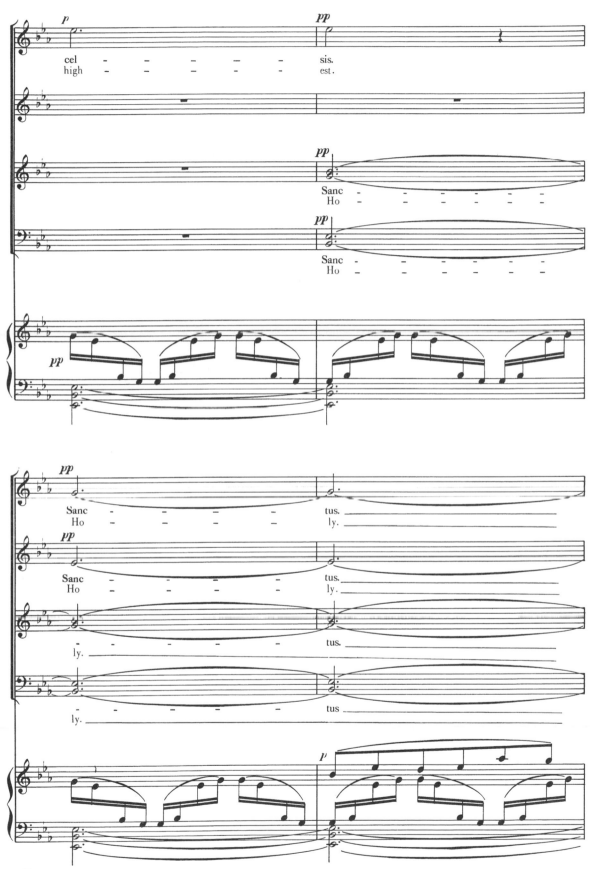

4. Pie Jesu
(Blessed Jesus)

5. Agnus Dei
(Lamb of God)

Ag - nus De - i qui tol - lis pec -
Lamb of God, _____ that tak - est a -

co - gi - ta mun - - di, Do -
way _____ the world's trans - gres - sions, Oh

A

na — e — is, do — na — e — is
grant, _____ oh grant, _____ oh _____ grant them e-

poco cresc.

Soprano

f

Ag - nus

o _____

Alto

f

Ag - nus

o _____

dim.

Tenor

f

re - qui - -em.
ter - - nal rest.

Ag - nus

o _____

Bass

f

Ag - nus

o _____

B

p

f

B

ce - at, lu - ce - at e - is.
on them, shine down up - on them.

ce - at, lu - ce - at e - is.
on them, shine down up - on ————— them.

ce - at, lu - ce - at e - is.
on them, shine down up - on ————— them.

ce - at, lu - ce - at e - is.
on them, shine down up - on ————— them.

6. Libera me

(Save my soul, Lord)

men - - - da,_____ in di - e il - -
judg - ment,_____ up on the day _____ of

la, Quan - do cae - li mo - ven - di
trial; When the heav . en and earth shall be

B

sunt, quan - do cae - li mo - ven di sunt et
moved, When the heav'n and earth shall be moved, be

crescendo

cresc.

ter - ra Dum ve - ne - ris ju - di
mov - ed; When Thou _____ shalt come, in the

sempre f

sempre f

cae - li mo - ven - di sunt et ter - ra
heav'n and earth shall be moved, be mov - ed;

cresc.

f

ff Dum ve - ne - ris ju - di - ca -
When Thou shalt come in the midst

7. In Paradisum

(Be thou in paradise)

tu - o ad - ven - tu sus - ci - pi - ant te
com - ing at - tend - ed by all the bless - ed

mar - ty - res,
mar - tyrs;

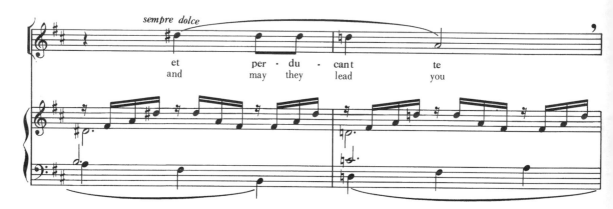

sempre dolce

et per - du - cant te
and may they lead you

in ci - vi - ta - tem sanc - tam, Je -
in - to the Ho - ly Cit - y, Je -

74

43966

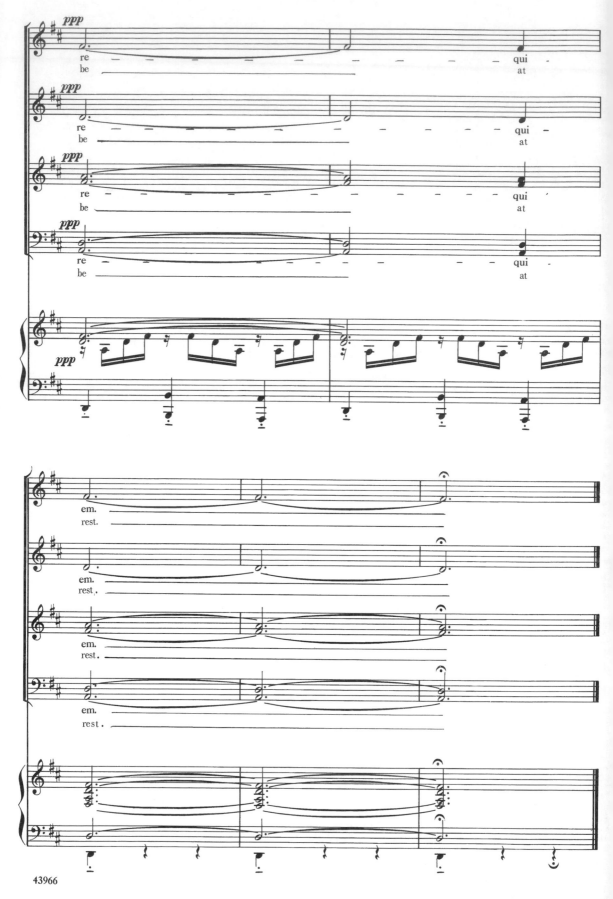